D0773576

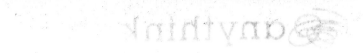

BASEBALL SMARTS

WHAT DOES A
CATCHER
DO?

Paul Challen

PowerKiDS
press™

New York

Published in 2017 by The Rosen Publishing Group, Inc.
29 East 21st Street, New York, NY 10010

Cataloging-in-Publication Data
Names: Challen, Paul.
Title: What does a catcher do? / Paul Challen.
Description: New York : PowerKids Press, 2017. | Series: Baseball smarts | Includes index.
Identifiers: ISBN 9781499432800 (pbk.) | ISBN 9781499432947 (library bound) |
   ISBN 9781499432930 (6 pack)
Subjects: LCSH: Catching (Baseball)--Juvenile literature.
Classification: LCC GV872.C53 2017 | DDC 796.357'23--dc23

Developed and Produced for Rosen by BlueApple*Works* Inc.
Managing Editor for BlueApple*Works*: Melissa McClellan
Art Director: Tibor Choleva
Designer: Joshua Avramson
Photo Research: Jane Reid
Editor: Marcia Abramson

Photo Credits: Cover Peter Lakomy/Shutterstock.com; page tops Photology1971/Shutterstock; title page middle, p. 7, 8, 18, 19 right Aspen Photo/Shutterstock; page bottoms Iasha/Shutterstock; TOC David Lee/Shutterstock; page backgrounds bottom Shawn Zhang /Shutterstock; page backgrounds top, p. 4 Eric Broder Van Dyke/Shutterstock; p. 9 Cheryl Ann Quigley/Shutterstock; p. 10 Chris Minor/Shutterstock; p. 11 Brian McEntire/iStockphoto; p. 12 Nero50/Dreamstime.com; p. 13, 17 right, 22 left, 28 Stephen Wise; p. 14 Aspenphoto/Dreamstime.com; p. 15 Sdbower/Dreamstime.com; p. 16 left tammykayphoto/Shutterstock; p. 16 right © Phfw22/Dreamstime.com; p. 17 left mTaira/Shutterstock; p. 19 left Matt_Brown/iStockphoto; p. 20, 21 Jamie Roach/Dreamstime. com; p. 22 right Scott Anderson/Dreamstime.com; p. 23 Keeton10/Dreamstime.com; p. 24, 27 top Jerry Coli/Dreamstime.com; p. 25 top, 27 left Keith Allison/Creative Commons; p. 25 bottom Theroff97/Dreamstime.com; p. 26 left Kevin Hill Illustration/ Shutterstock.com; p. 26 right Johnmaxmena2/Creative Commons; p. 29 left Debby Wong/Shutterstock.com; p. 29 top Kent Weakley/Shutterstock; back cover Eugene Onischenko/Shutterstock

Manufactured in the United States of America
CPSIA Compliance Information: Batch #BW17PK For Further Information contact: Rosen Publishing, New York, New York at 1-800-237-9932

CONTENTS

The Baseball Team   4
The Catcher   6
Strategy   8
Calling the Perfect Game   10
Catching the Pitch   12
Blocking Pitches   14
Throwing   16
Fielding Bunts   18
Tagging the Runner   20
Hitting the Ball   22
The Role of a Manager   24
The Best of the Catchers   26
Be a Good Sport   28
Glossary   30
For More Information   31
Index   32

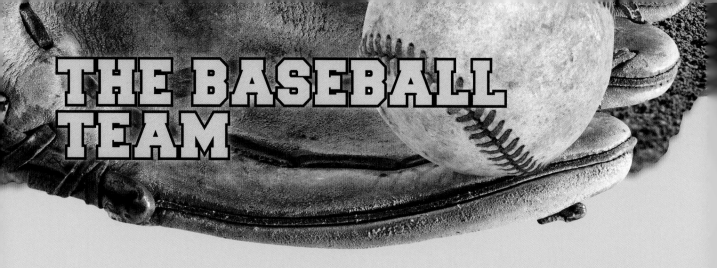

THE BASEBALL TEAM

Two teams go head-to-head in the action-packed sport of baseball. Each team fields nine players, and games are divided into innings. The teams switch between defense and offense each inning. On the offensive side, the team tries to score runs by hitting the ball and running the bases. Defensively, teams use pitching, catching, and throwing to try to stop the opponents from scoring.

All baseball infields are square in shape, but are known as "diamonds." Home plate and the three bases are on the corners of this diamond. The paths between each base are 90 feet (27.4 m) long. Right in the middle of the infield is the pitcher's mound, which is 60 feet, 6 inches (18.4 m) from home plate.

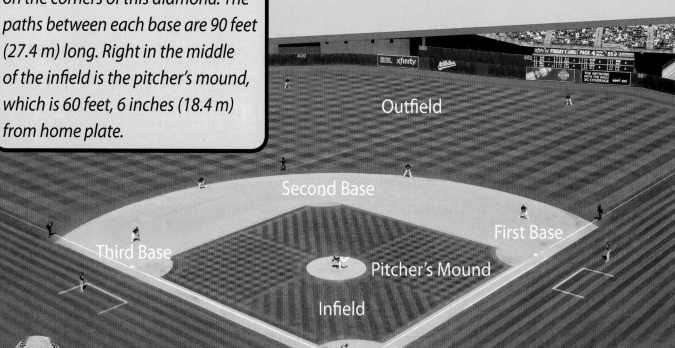

Outfield

Second Base

First Base

Third Base

Pitcher's Mound

Infield

Home Plate

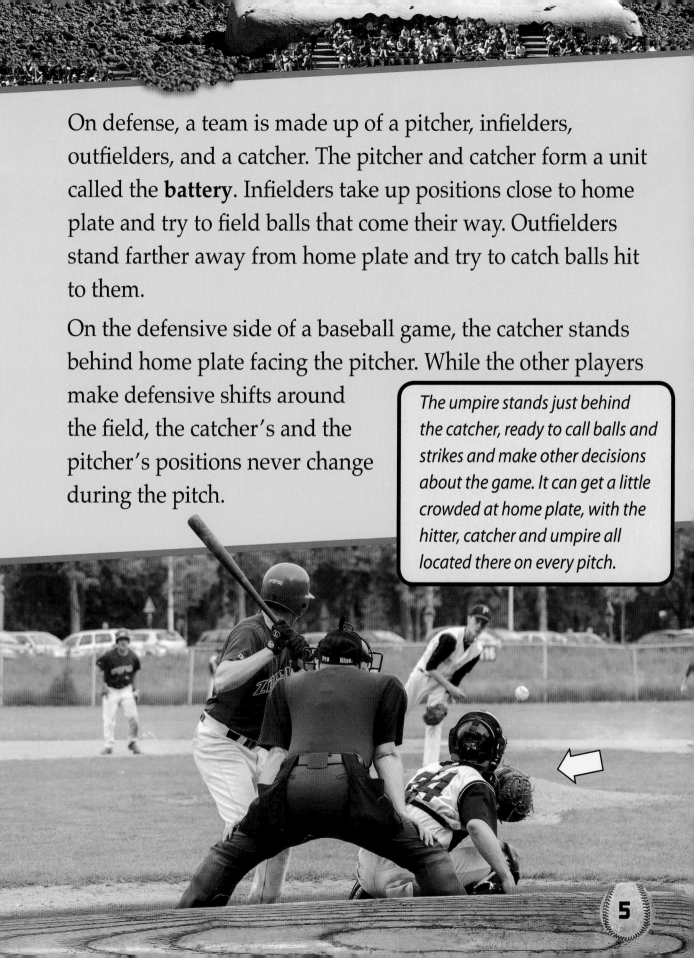

On defense, a team is made up of a pitcher, infielders, outfielders, and a catcher. The pitcher and catcher form a unit called the **battery**. Infielders take up positions close to home plate and try to field balls that come their way. Outfielders stand farther away from home plate and try to catch balls hit to them.

On the defensive side of a baseball game, the catcher stands behind home plate facing the pitcher. While the other players make defensive shifts around the field, the catcher's and the pitcher's positions never change during the pitch.

The umpire stands just behind the catcher, ready to call balls and strikes and make other decisions about the game. It can get a little crowded at home plate, with the hitter, catcher and umpire all located there on every pitch.

THE CATCHER

The catcher has a very important position on a baseball team. The main job of this player is to catch balls thrown past the batter by the pitcher. On every pitch, the catcher waits in a squatting or **crouching** position behind the plate. Catchers place their glove where the pitcher is aiming to throw the ball as a target. The catcher and the pitcher work together using special **signs** to decide what kind of pitch the pitcher will deliver.

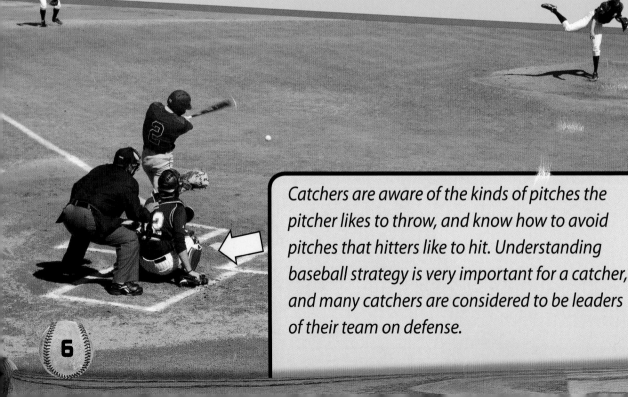

Catchers are aware of the kinds of pitches the pitcher likes to throw, and know how to avoid pitches that hitters like to hit. Understanding baseball strategy is very important for a catcher, and many catchers are considered to be leaders of their team on defense.

The catcher plays a part in two important baseball statistics— the wild pitch and the passed ball. Both of these stats come from a pitcher's throw to home plate, and happen when a catcher fails to catch the ball, resulting in a runner advancing from one base to another. It is then up to the official game scorer to determine if the catcher should have been able to catch the ball with normal effort. If the scorer decides the catcher should have, the play is recorded as a passed ball. If the catcher could not have been expected to catch it, a wild pitch is recorded.

FIELDING

Catchers must also cover home plate on defensive plays. This includes catching pop-up hits, foul tips that come straight off a hitter's bat, and **bunts** that are hit a short distance. Another responsibility of the catcher is covering home plate on balls thrown home in an attempt to force or **tag** out a runner. These plays sometimes end in collisions between the runner and the catcher.

Because of all the action at the plate, a catcher wears a lot of protective equipment. This includes a special mask, helmet, shin guards, a chest protector, and a throat protector. As well, the catcher wears a glove different from that of any other player. A **catcher's mitt** has heavy padding and is specially designed to catch pitches.

STRATEGY

Understanding the ins and outs of baseball is very important for a catcher. As well as knowing the different habits of pitchers and hitters, the catcher must study the position of the fielders and base runners, and be prepared to make fast decisions on every play.

The catcher must also understand the mental game of baseball. If a pitcher is becoming rattled after giving up hits or throwing a lot of poor pitches, the catcher is the one who must calm the pitcher down.

Catchers also work closely with baseball coaches to determine strategy on the field and are often considered "coaches on the field" because of this aspect of their game.

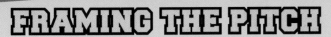

FRAMING THE PITCH

One important tool a catcher can use to help a pitcher is known as **framing** a pitch. Using this technique, a catcher holds the mitt right at the edge of the strike zone and gives the pitcher this target to aim at. If the pitcher can hit it, the umpire may consider the pitch a strike. Even if the pitch is called a ball, the next time the pitcher hits this frame the umpire may consider it a strike.

Catchers also use tricks like catching a pitch just outside the strike zone and carefully moving their mitts just inside the strike zone before the umpire has a chance to make a call. Again, this is an attempt to persuade the umpire to call a strike on a pitch that might have been a ball.

Good catchers have quick feet and good flexibility. They also need a strong throwing arm and the physical strength to face many different situations on the field.

9

CALLING THE PERFECT GAME

Maybe the most important job a catcher can do is known as **calling the game**. Good catchers will know the habits of a batter so well, they can determine the right pitch for the pitcher to throw at any given time. Depending on the situation, the catcher will call for a fastball, curve ball, slider, or several other types of pitch to be thrown. Catchers use special finger signs to call for these pitches.

As well as the type of pitch, catchers also call for the location of a pitch. For example, a catcher may call for a fastball to be delivered to the high and inside part of the strike zone.

A pitcher can always refuse the catcher's call on any pitch and ask for a different sign. If they can't agree sometimes they will have a meeting on the mound.

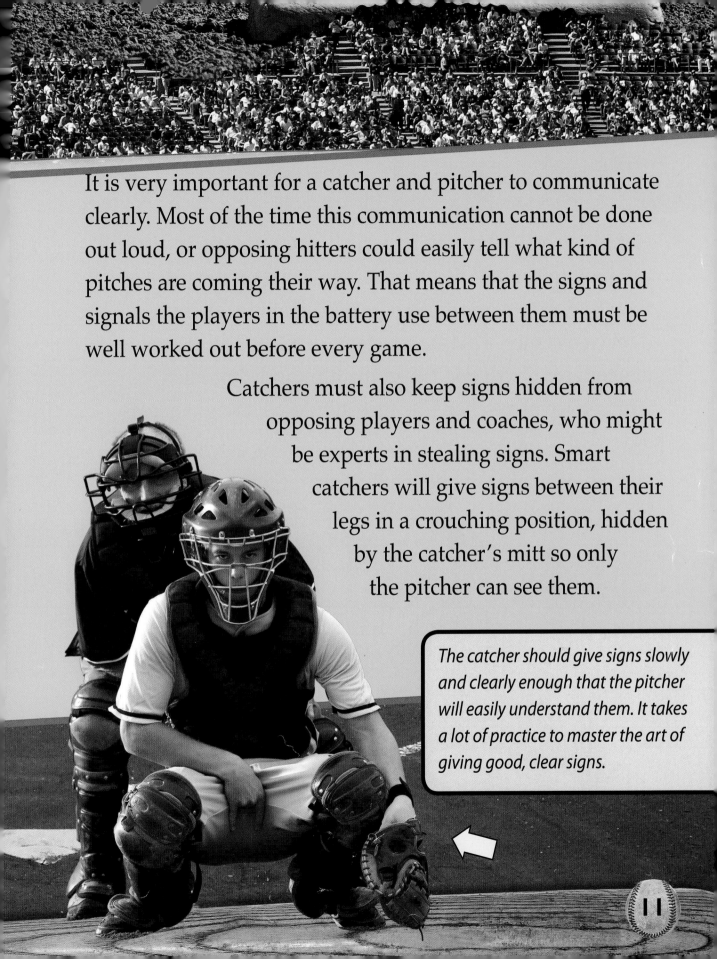

It is very important for a catcher and pitcher to communicate clearly. Most of the time this communication cannot be done out loud, or opposing hitters could easily tell what kind of pitches are coming their way. That means that the signs and signals the players in the battery use between them must be well worked out before every game.

Catchers must also keep signs hidden from opposing players and coaches, who might be experts in stealing signs. Smart catchers will give signs between their legs in a crouching position, hidden by the catcher's mitt so only the pitcher can see them.

The catcher should give signs slowly and clearly enough that the pitcher will easily understand them. It takes a lot of practice to master the art of giving good, clear signs.

CATCHING THE PITCH

Getting in a good position to catch a pitch is key to actually catching the ball. When there are no base runners and less than two strikes, most catchers use what is known as a relaxed stance. This stance starts with the feet placed at shoulder width apart, and the hips and shoulders squared to the pitcher. The feet should be straight across.

The important thing in this stance—or any catcher's stance—is to give the pitcher a good target to aim at.

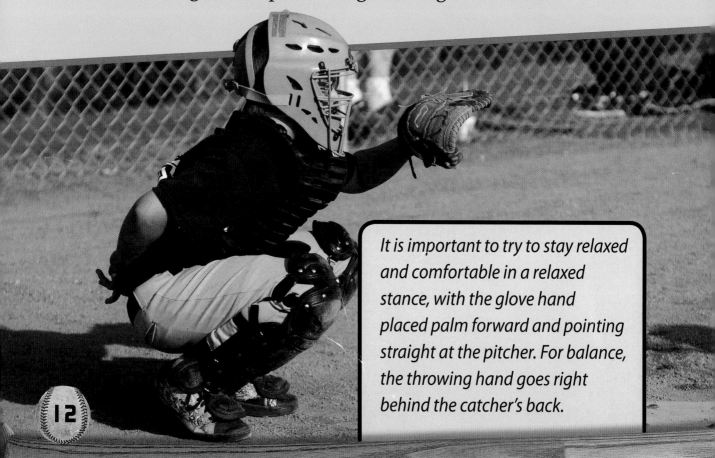

It is important to try to stay relaxed and comfortable in a relaxed stance, with the glove hand placed palm forward and pointing straight at the pitcher. For balance, the throwing hand goes right behind the catcher's back.

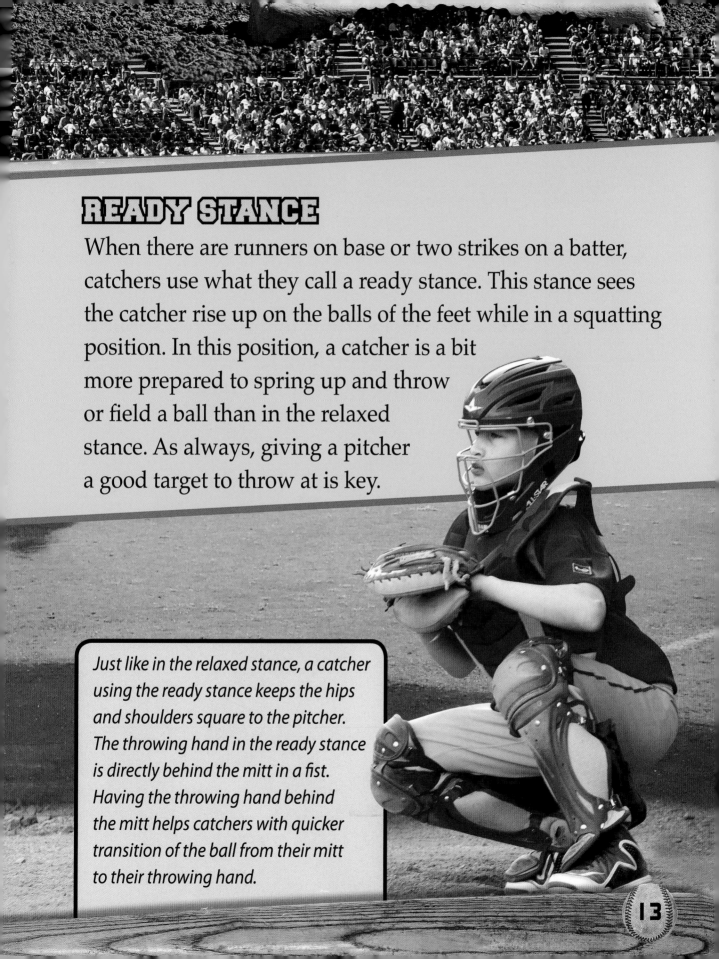

READY STANCE

When there are runners on base or two strikes on a batter, catchers use what they call a ready stance. This stance sees the catcher rise up on the balls of the feet while in a squatting position. In this position, a catcher is a bit more prepared to spring up and throw or field a ball than in the relaxed stance. As always, giving a pitcher a good target to throw at is key.

Just like in the relaxed stance, a catcher using the ready stance keeps the hips and shoulders square to the pitcher. The throwing hand in the ready stance is directly behind the mitt in a fist. Having the throwing hand behind the mitt helps catchers with quicker transition of the ball from their mitt to their throwing hand.

BLOCKING PITCHES

A successful catcher must also know how to **block** pitches thrown too low that hit the dirt around home plate. Of course, pitchers are usually trying to throw strikes, but sometimes pitches get away from them and end up in the dirt. If such a pitch gets past the catcher, the ball can travel a long way past home plate, allowing base runners to advance and sometimes even score.

Coaches teach catchers to keep the ball in front of them in any way possible, which can mean letting the ball bounce off the chest protector, shin protectors, or even the mask.

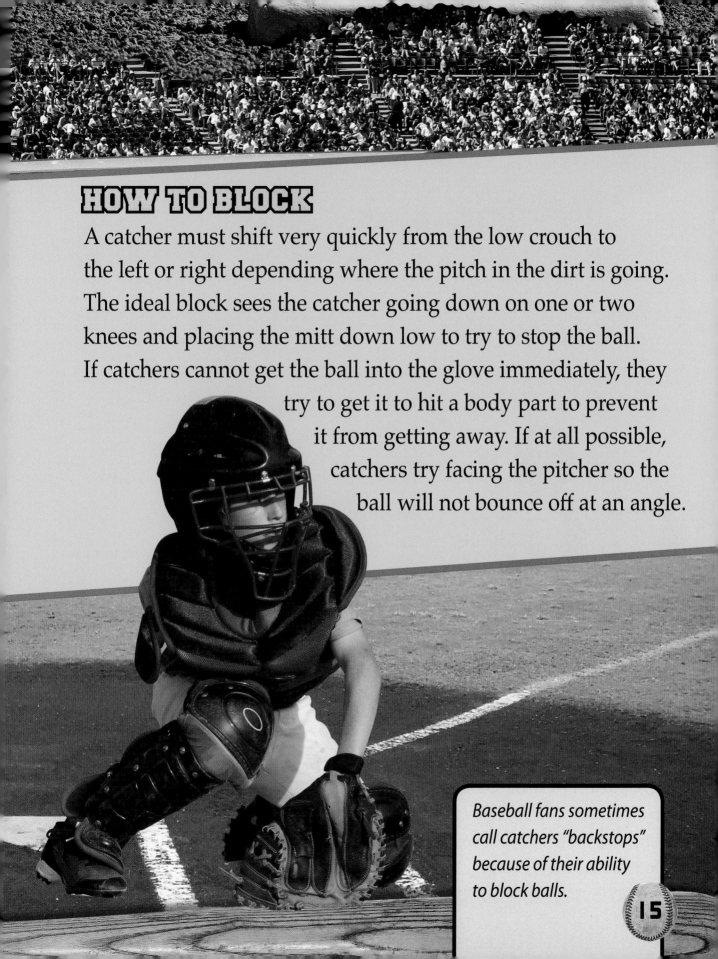

HOW TO BLOCK

A catcher must shift very quickly from the low crouch to the left or right depending where the pitch in the dirt is going. The ideal block sees the catcher going down on one or two knees and placing the mitt down low to try to stop the ball. If catchers cannot get the ball into the glove immediately, they try to get it to hit a body part to prevent it from getting away. If at all possible, catchers try facing the pitcher so the ball will not bounce off at an angle.

Baseball fans sometimes call catchers "backstops" because of their ability to block balls.

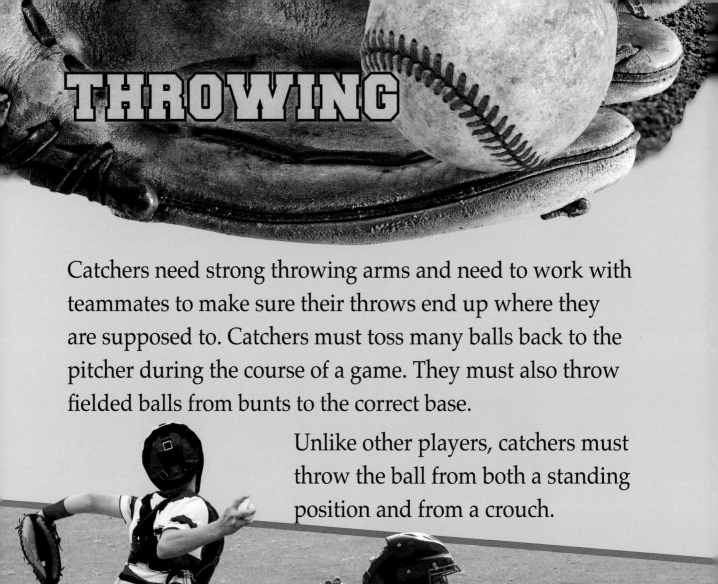

THROWING

Catchers need strong throwing arms and need to work with teammates to make sure their throws end up where they are supposed to. Catchers must toss many balls back to the pitcher during the course of a game. They must also throw fielded balls from bunts to the correct base.

Unlike other players, catchers must throw the ball from both a standing position and from a crouch.

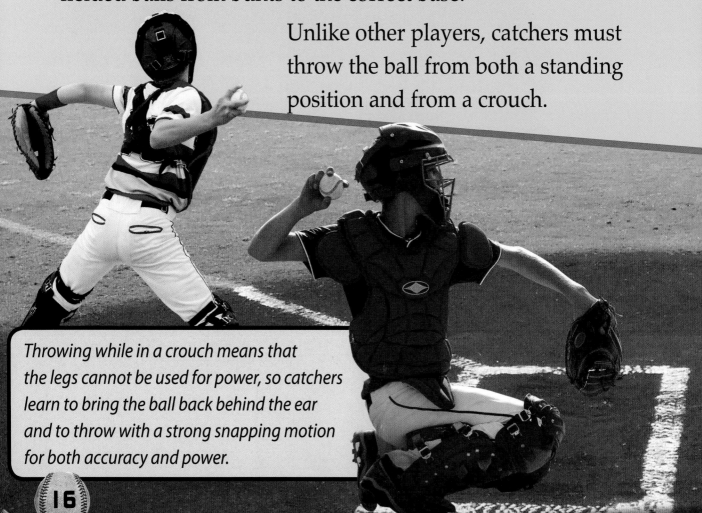

Throwing while in a crouch means that the legs cannot be used for power, so catchers learn to bring the ball back behind the ear and to throw with a strong snapping motion for both accuracy and power.

STEALING

A catcher who can successfully throw out runners trying to **steal bases** will help the defensive team in a big way. To throw out a runner, a catcher must **receive** a pitch that a hitter fails to make contact with. The catcher then jumps up out of the crouching position, and has to deliver a fast, accurate throw to the teammate covering the base the runner is attempting to steal. If the throw is on target, the infielder can catch it and tag the runner out. But if the catcher's throw hits the base runner, the runner will be called safe by the umpire. And if the throw sails over the base, the runner can continue on and try to steal another base. So accuracy is key!

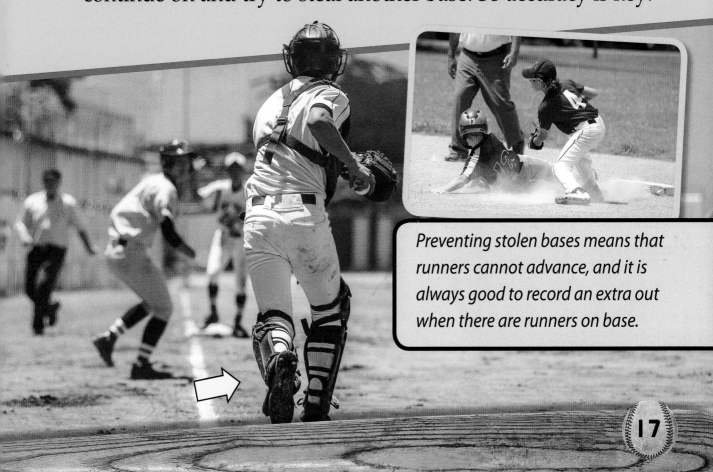

Preventing stolen bases means that runners cannot advance, and it is always good to record an extra out when there are runners on base.

FIELDING BUNTS

When a batter decides not to take a full swing but rather just to let the ball hit the bat in an attempt to make it roll a short distance, it is called a bunt. The catcher is sometimes the player in the best position to field the bunt. Catchers must scoop the ball up quickly and throw it to the correct base as quickly as possible. It is important not to bobble or drop the ball before throwing it, which may allow a hitter time to reach first base, or other runners time to reach theirs.

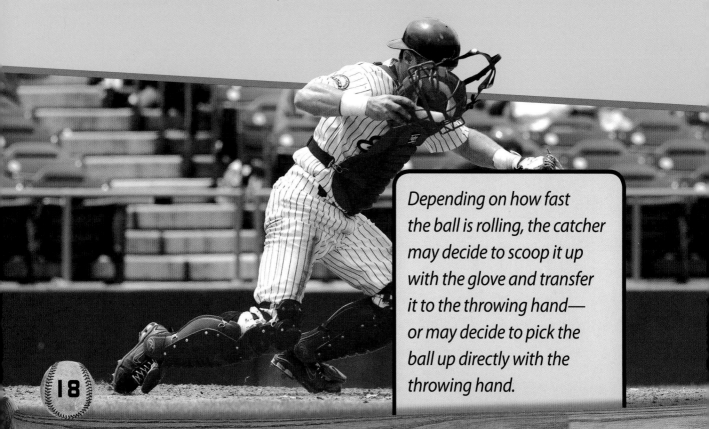

Depending on how fast the ball is rolling, the catcher may decide to scoop it up with the glove and transfer it to the throwing hand—or may decide to pick the ball up directly with the throwing hand.

POP-UPS

Catchers are also responsible for catching pop-ups hit in fair or foul territory near home plate. This can be very tough to do, as it is hard to come up out of a crouch and locate a ball hit very high up in the air. If a catcher can locate the ball and it seems likely he can make the catch, it is very important to call for the ball and let other teammates know to back off.

A catcher should run to the spot where the ball will drop, and take off the catcher's mask to make it easier to see the ball.

TAGGING THE RUNNER

Tagging a runner at home plate is one of a catcher's most exciting plays—and sometimes the most exciting play in an entire game. Since a runner who touches home plate without being tagged scores a run, making the tag is especially important. These runners may try to slide past the catcher to touch home plate with a foot or hand, or may take the direct route to tag home plate and slam into the catcher in an attempt to get him to drop the ball, making a tag impossible.

A catcher cannot block a base runner's path to home plate if the catcher does not have the ball. Without the ball, the catcher must allow the runner a clear path to home plate.

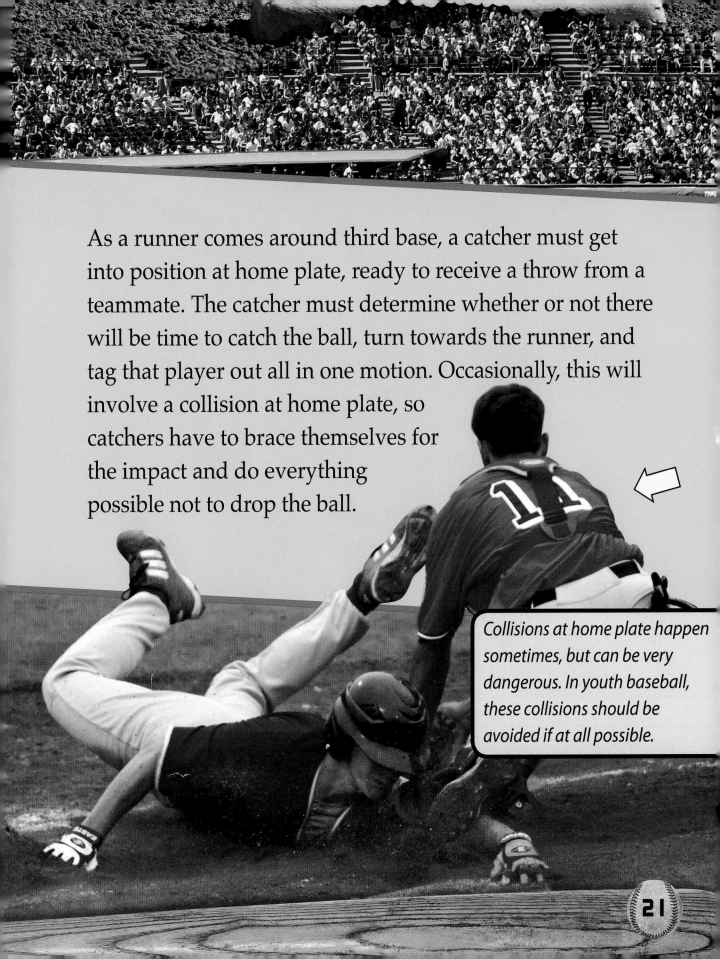

As a runner comes around third base, a catcher must get into position at home plate, ready to receive a throw from a teammate. The catcher must determine whether or not there will be time to catch the ball, turn towards the runner, and tag that player out all in one motion. Occasionally, this will involve a collision at home plate, so catchers have to brace themselves for the impact and do everything possible not to drop the ball.

Collisions at home plate happen sometimes, but can be very dangerous. In youth baseball, these collisions should be avoided if at all possible.

HITTING THE BALL

On the offensive side of the game, catchers must contribute to their team with good hitting. Many catchers in Major League Baseball are among their teams' best hitters. Because they have a great understanding of the strike zone and know how to "read" pitchers, catchers can often be counted on to be both long-ball power hitters and contact hitters who know how to get on base with shorter hits.

Just like any player, catchers must practice hitting constantly to stay sharp and refine their swing. They need to know how to hit all kinds of pitches with different spins and at different speeds.

DID YOU KNOW?

In baseball terms, the player who is at home plate and batting is "at the plate," "at bat," or "up to bat." Many fans simply say that such a player is "up." While a hitter is up, the next player due to bat waits in an area known as the on-deck circle, between the team dugout and home plate. Fans say this waiting player is "on deck." The player who hits after the on-deck player is said to be "in the hole." Of course, if a player at bat makes a third out, the on-deck and "hole" players must wait until the next inning to get their chance to hit.

Because catchers are so important to a team's defense, the players at this position are usually chosen by managers for their defensive skills, rather than their hitting. This means that catchers who can hit well are extremely valuable to any team, because they can contribute offense to a team as well as make a difference on defense.

Because of the athletic abilities needed to be a good catcher, these players are often power hitters, capable of hitting lots of home runs and driving in lots of runs.

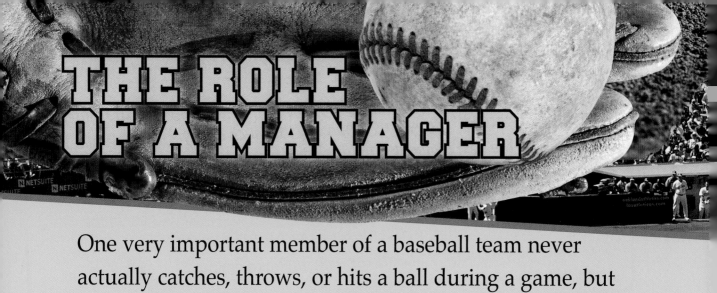

THE ROLE OF A MANAGER

One very important member of a baseball team never actually catches, throws, or hits a ball during a game, but is key to the team's success. This is the manager, whose job is similar to the head coach in sports such as football, basketball, or hockey. The manager determines the team's strategy from inside the dugout. The manager's job can include deciding which players to put in the defensive positions on the field, in what order the batters should hit, and who should pitch.

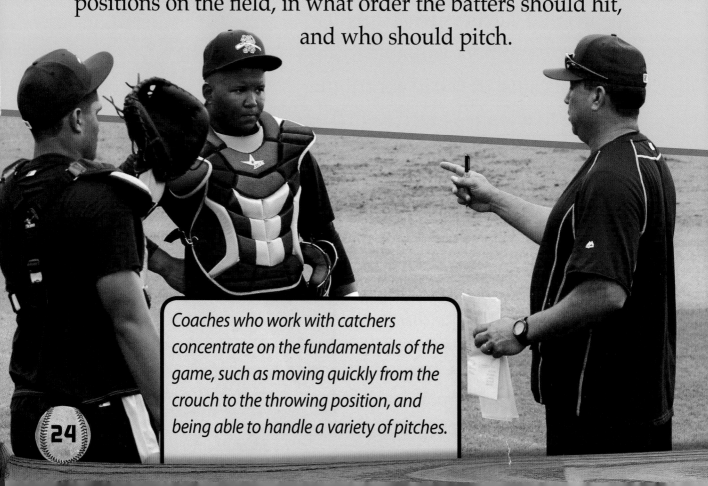

Coaches who work with catchers concentrate on the fundamentals of the game, such as moving quickly from the crouch to the throwing position, and being able to handle a variety of pitches.

Many baseball catchers become managers when their playing careers are over. Because catchers are so involved in a team's strategy on the field, they have the perfect background for making decisions from the bench. For example, the New York Yankees' current manager, Joe Girardi, played this position for several major league teams. Girardi caught for the Chicago Cubs, Colorado Rockies, St. Louis Cardinals, and the Yankees themselves. In 2006, while managing the Florida Marlins, Girardi was named the National League Manager of the Year.

COACHES ON THE FIELD

Managers do not do their job alone. They are assisted by a team of coaches who work with players on certain aspects of the game. For example, pitching coaches work with pitchers to develop their skills, and hitting or batting coaches help offensive players work on their swing and make contact with the ball.

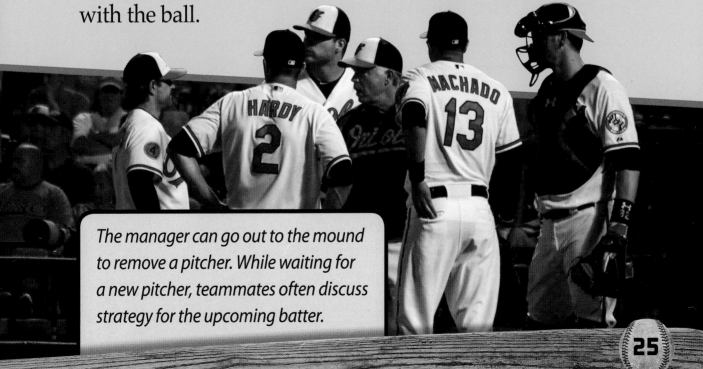

The manager can go out to the mound to remove a pitcher. While waiting for a new pitcher, teammates often discuss strategy for the upcoming batter.

THE BEST OF THE CATCHERS

There have been many famed catchers in baseball history. Carlton Fisk played in the majors from 1969 to 1993, and hit 351 home runs in his career with the Boston Red Sox and Chicago White Sox. Legendary New York Yankees catcher Yogi Berra was well-loved by fans for his great sense of humor. He was an 18-time All-Star and won the World Series 10 times. Ivan Rodriguez, who played for six different teams in the majors from 1991 to 2011, is considered by most fans to be the best defensive catcher of all time.

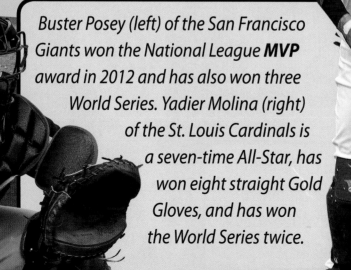

Buster Posey (left) of the San Francisco Giants won the National League **MVP** award in 2012 and has also won three World Series. Yadier Molina (right) of the St. Louis Cardinals is a seven-time All-Star, has won eight straight Gold Gloves, and has won the World Series twice.

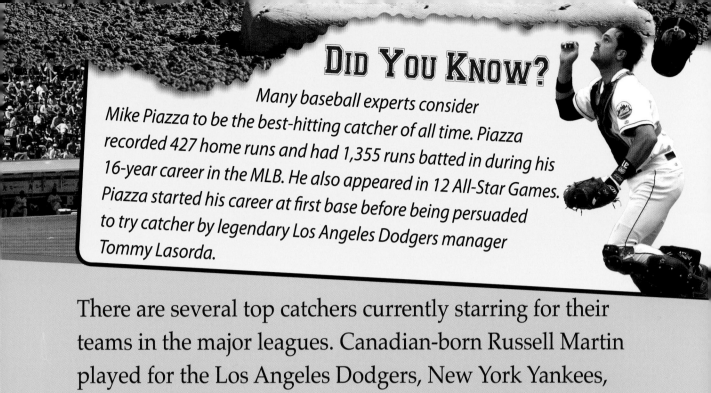

There are several top catchers currently starring for their teams in the major leagues. Canadian-born Russell Martin played for the Los Angeles Dodgers, New York Yankees, and Pittsburgh Pirates before his current team, the Toronto Blue Jays. Martin won the 2007 National League Gold Glove Award for best defensive catcher. Jonathan Lucroy of the Texas Rangers, formerly of the Milwaukee Brewers, was a 2014 All-Star. Stephen Vogt is a popular member of the Oakland Athletics. Fans sing a special "I Believe in Stephen Vogt" chant every time he comes to bat.

The Kansas City Royals' Salvador Perez is a three-time Gold Glove winner, and has been an All-Star four times. When his team won the 2015 World Series, Perez was named MVP.

BE A GOOD SPORT

Every player wants to win in baseball, but fair play, good sportsmanship, and respect for the game are also very important. Shaking hands after a game, encouraging teammates and opponents during the action, and taking care of yourself and your equipment are all key to making baseball the great game it is. Even major league players know that being a good sport is vital.

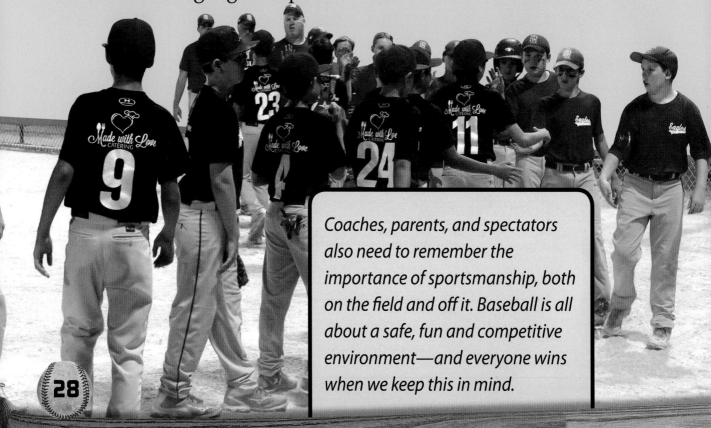

Coaches, parents, and spectators also need to remember the importance of sportsmanship, both on the field and off it. Baseball is all about a safe, fun and competitive environment—and everyone wins when we keep this in mind.

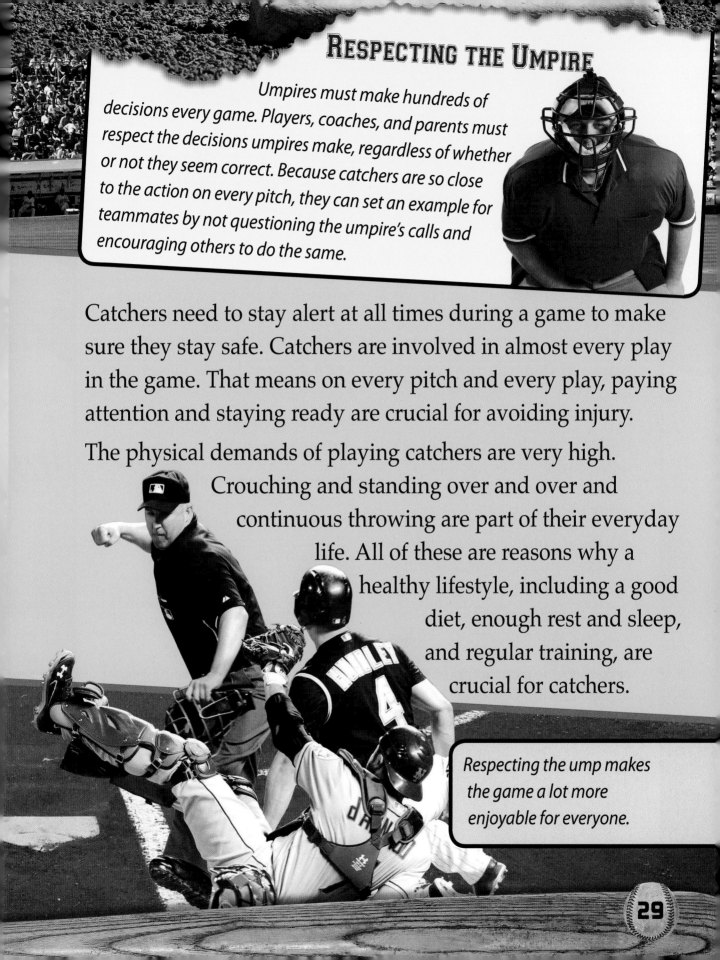

RESPECTING THE UMPIRE

Umpires must make hundreds of decisions every game. Players, coaches, and parents must respect the decisions umpires make, regardless of whether or not they seem correct. Because catchers are so close to the action on every pitch, they can set an example for teammates by not questioning the umpire's calls and encouraging others to do the same.

Catchers need to stay alert at all times during a game to make sure they stay safe. Catchers are involved in almost every play in the game. That means on every pitch and every play, paying attention and staying ready are crucial for avoiding injury.

The physical demands of playing catchers are very high. Crouching and standing over and over and continuous throwing are part of their everyday life. All of these are reasons why a healthy lifestyle, including a good diet, enough rest and sleep, and regular training, are crucial for catchers.

Respecting the ump makes the game a lot more enjoyable for everyone.

GLOSSARY

battery The combination of a pitcher and catcher on a baseball team.

block To stop balls thrown in the dirt by pitchers, in whatever way necessary.

bunt A short hit accomplished when a hitter does not take a full swing but instead just lets a pitch hit the bat.

calling a game The decisions a catcher makes regarding pitch selection.

catcher's mitt The special baseball glove used by a catcher.

crouch To lower the body to the ground by bending the legs. Also, the special stance used by a baseball catcher.

framing A catcher's technique that helps a pitcher locate the edges of a batter's strike zone.

MVP Most Valuable Player, a baseball honor.

receive To catch pitches thrown by a pitcher.

signs The finger signals a catcher sends to a pitcher to determine pitch choice.

steal (a base) To attempt to run safely to the next base as an offensive player after a pitch that has not been hit fair or foul.

tag To put a runner out by touching them with the ball or with the glove that has the ball in it before they have reached a base.

FOR MORE INFORMATION

FURTHER READING

Dreier, David. *Baseball: How It Works.*
Mankato, MN: Capstone Press, 2011.

Editors of Sports Illustrated Kids. *Sports Illustrated Kids Full Count.*
New York: Sports Illustrated, 2012.

Fishman, Jon. *Buster Posey.*
Minneapolis, MN: Lerner Classroom, 2016.

LeBoutillier, Nate. *The Best of Everything Baseball Book.*
Mankato, MN: Capstone Press, 2011.

WEBSITES

Due to the changing nature of Internet links, PowerKids Press has
developed an online list of websites related to the subject of this book.
This site is updated regularly. Please use this link to access the list:

www.powerkidslinks.com/bs/catcher

INDEX

B
balls and strikes 5
battery 5, 11
block 14, 15, 20
bunts 7, 16, 18

C
catcher's mitt 7, 11
catching 4, 7, 9, 12, 19
chest protector 7, 14
coaches 8, 11, 14, 24, 25, 28, 29

D
defense 4, 5, 6, 23

F
fastball 10
framing 9

G
glove 6, 7, 12, 15, 18

H
hitting 4, 22, 23, 25, 27
home plate 4, 5, 7, 14, 19, 20, 21, 23

I
infielders 5
innings 4

M
Major League Baseball (MLB) 22
manager 24, 25, 27
Molina, Yadier 26

O
offense 4, 23
outfielders 5

P
Perez, Salvador 27
Piazza, Mike 27
pitcher 4, 5, 6, 7, 8, 9, 10, 11, 12, 13, 15, 16, 19, 25
pitching 4, 25
pop-ups 7, 19
Posey, Buster 26

R
ready stance 13
relaxed stance 12, 13

S
signs 6, 10, 11
stolen bases 17
strike zone 9, 10, 22

T
tag 7, 17, 19, 20, 21
throwing 4, 8, 9, 12, 13, 16, 18, 24, 29

U
umpire 5, 9, 17, 29